Depression

How To Stop Worrying, Relieve Anxiety And Eliminate Negative Thinking

UNLEASH YOUR INNER GREATNESS

Copyright 2016 by Robert Waden - All rights reserved.

This document is geared towards providing exact and reliable information in regards to the topic and issue covered. The publication is sold with the idea that the publisher is not required to render accounting, officially permitted, or otherwise, qualified services. If advice is necessary, legal or professional, a practiced individual in the profession should be ordered.

- From a Declaration of Principles which was accepted and approved equally by a Committee of the American Bar Association and a Committee of Publishers and Associations.

In no way is it legal to reproduce, duplicate, or transmit any part of this document in either electronic means or in printed format. Recording of this publication is strictly prohibited and any storage of this document is not allowed unless with written permission from the publisher. All rights reserved.

The information provided herein is stated to be truthful and consistent, in that any liability, in terms of inattention or otherwise, by any usage or abuse of any policies, processes, or directions contained within is the solitary and utter responsibility of the recipient reader. Under no circumstances will any legal responsibility or blame be held against the publisher for any reparation, damages, or monetary loss due to the information herein, either directly or indirectly.

Respective authors own all copyrights not held by the publisher.

The information herein is offered for informational purposes solely, and is universal as so. The presentation of the information is without contract or any type of guarantee assurance.

The trademarks that are used are without any consent, and the publication of the trademark is without permission or backing by the trademark owner. All trademarks and brands within this book are for clarifying purposes only and are the owned by the owners themselves, not affiliated with this document.

TABLE OF CONTENTS

WHAT IS DEPRESSION?..1

WHAT CAUSES DEPRESSION..................................9

DIFFERENT FORMS OF DEPRESSION....................17

HOW DEPRESSION AFFECTS THE SUFFERER AND THOSE AROUND HIM OR HER...............................25

DEALING WITH GUILT..33

DEALING WITH A LACK OF SELF-ESTEEM...........36

DEALING WITH "ALL OR NOTHING" THINKING ..41

DEALING WITH HOPELESS THINKING 44

DEALING WITH PERSISTENT SADNESS................47

DEALING WITH A LACK OF INTEREST 50

DEPRESSION FREE METHOD: LEARNING NEW THINKING FOR NEW BEHAVIOR 53

MEDICATIONS EXPLAINED IN PLAIN ENGLISH ...59

DEPRESSION FREE METHOD 10-STEP ACTION PLAN TO OVERCOMING YOUR DEPRESSION 66

WHAT IS DEPRESSION?

There is probably no one alive that has not been depressed at one time or another in their life. In simple terms, depression just refers to a period of sadness, gloominess, or dejection. It's easy to understand how anyone can feel these emotions at one time or another - the death of a friend or family member, the loss of a job, marital and other family problems, and just plain stresses from the world we live in can make anyone sad and gloomy for some time. Even a day of bad weather can make one feel a bit gloomy!

But what is meant by depression? Why and how is it different than these "normal" times of sadness, and why is it important for someone that suffers from this condition to consider this information?

CLINICAL DEPRESSION

When we talk about depression, it's important to understand that we are not talking about these typical periods of sadness or gloominess that everyone suffers from one time or another. It's important to understand the difference between normal periods of sadness and actual clinical depression. Let's outline these differences here.

Temporary versus permanent.

If you lose someone in death, or lose your job, or go through some other traumatic experience of course you're going to feel sad and upset. But for the most part, these feeling subside in time and after adjustments are made. While you may of course never get over someone's death, you do eventually move on with your life. Jobs can be replaced, divorces put behind you, and so on.

Clinical depression however is not some temporary feeling that just subsides or goes away based on whether or not a person is going through a temporary situation or set of circumstances. Clinical depression is chronic and consistent and doesn't subside so easily.

Based on circumstances.

If you've been through any type of negative or stressful event and come out of it feeling depressed and gloomy, then you can easily pinpoint the cause of your depression. A job loss, a divorce, a death, surviving a traumatic event such as a crime or natural disaster, and things like these are when the depression started for those suffering from "normal" depression.

But with clinical depression, there is rarely a particular reason or circumstance that causes it. Sufferers can rarely go back to an event or reason for their feelings.

This isn't a hard and fast rule, however. Some who suffer from clinical depression have found that it was triggered by one particular circumstance and that they perhaps did not have the necessary emotional tools to deal with this event or to recover from it afterwards. Because of this, their emotional state began something of a downward spiral that has pulled them into a state of clinical depression and which they will need assistance with before they can recover.

Depths of feelings.

If you're feeling sad and depressed because you've lost a job, that's perfectly understandable. You may also be experiencing a range of other emotions that are making the situation worse, such as fear for the future and how you'll pay your bills, anger at the person or situation that caused you to lose your job, frustration at the job market, and irritation that you even need to be out looking for a job right now.

All of these feelings are perfectly natural and to be expected, but rarely does someone feel suicidal because of a job loss, or divorce or other circumstance, at least not for an extended period of time and not in a way that really puts their life in danger. An unemployed or recently divorced person may have times when they just don't want to get out of bed, but a person that is truly clinically depressed feels this way all the time and to such depths that these feelings interfere with all their activities all the time.

A person that has true clinical depression feels not just sad but hopeless, uninterested in daily life, hobbies, family, friends, and things that had previously interested him or her, and typically has a problem enjoying virtually anything about their life or activities.

Clinical depression can also be so overwhelming that it affects a person's habits, their career, their decision making abilities, their sleeping and eating habits, and their sexual habits as well.

SYMPTOMS OF CLINICAL DEPRESSION

How do you know if you are clinically depressed or if you're just going through a "bad patch"? Obviously speaking to a healthcare professional is always recommended as only he or she can actually give you an accurate diagnosis, but there are some things you can keep in mind to decide whether or not you should speak to your doctor.

Loss of interest.

Probably the most common symptom and the one that affects a patient of clinical depression the most is their loss of interest in everyday activities, friends, family, hobbies, and things they even once used to enjoy. This loss of interest is usually manifest in the following ways:

It affects all aspects of a person's life; this makes it different than just general burnout that one might experience from being in a stressful career for a long time, or when someone simply gets tired of a hobby, relationship, and so on.

It affects things that a person typically would enjoy or has enjoyed in the past, including hobbies, religious pursuits, and even things such as exercise or sexual activity.

It affects one's relationships even with those they are closest to; they have a hard time working up interest in their children's activities, their family members, and so on. Mood swings. Everyone gets moody from time to time and may experience different moods depending on where they are and what they are doing; it's common for many to feel a bit depressed on Sunday night as they realize that Monday is just around the corner, and this mood lightens sometime around Thursday night as the weekend gets closer.

But for those who have clinical depression, mood swings are a persistent and chronic part of their everyday experience and rarely has anything to do with external circumstances. They may have a hard time getting out of bed one day and then feel a sudden burst of energy the next. Or the most trivial thing can trigger their anger or a sudden outburst, such as an innocent question from a child or a preempted television program.

Persistent feeling of sadness.

Another of the most common symptoms of clinical depression is the constant and chronic feeling of sadness that one experiences. This means that a person can feel sad even when at a happy event such as a family reunion or wedding, or can feel sad watching a movie, and so on. It seems that with clinical depression even everyday events can make one sad, such as grocery shopping, preparing meals, and so on.

This persistent feeling of sadness can also be considering a feeling of hopelessness or lack of drive and motivation for even the smallest things; the thought of "what's the use?" seems to pervade the thinking of someone with clinical depression, even when doing necessary chores and daily activities. They just aren't "motivated" to do the grocery shopping or respond to the boss' email or return a phone call. Not only do they lack the motivation to do these even mundane or habitual tasks, they often find that these things seem to just aggravate their feelings of sadness overall.

Other symptoms.

Clinical depression has different symptoms for every person, just like grief or anger or irritation is going to express itself differently for everyone. Here are some other common symptoms of clinical depression:

A consistent "empty" feeling.

Change in eating patterns, such as suddenly constantly overeating or losing all interest in food.

Extreme patterns in sleep or sleeplessness; this includes insomnia, persistently waking up too early and being unable to get back to sleep, oversleeping, sleeping for extended periods in the day.

Chronic restlessness or irritability; outbursts of anger and/or crying jags.

Inappropriate negative emotions, such as feelings of guilt, helplessness, frustration, being trapped, extreme pessimism.

Difficulty thinking and concentrating; typically unable to make decisions or chronically avoiding decision making. Sufferers often seem to be very "distracted" and mentally burdened.

Withdrawal from family, friends, and virtually all social situations.

Panic attacks.

Extreme fatigue, sluggishness, and sleepiness.

PHYSICAL SYMPTOMS

While depression is a mental and emotional illness, it can affect a patient physically. Symptoms of depression that appear physically include chronic headaches, stomachaches, indigestion, acne, muscle or stomach cramps, dry skin, nausea, and consistent pain for no apparent reason. It's also interesting that many persons suffering from clinical depression also seem to suffer from a loss of certain motor control functions in that they often become somewhat clumsy. They often find that physical activities they once enjoyed become cumbersome; even playing favorite sports, dancing, and activities like this are suddenly very difficult for them.

There are many reasons as to why a condition such as depression would cause physical problems in the sufferer; it's believed that because the body produces an excess of stress hormones when one is under duress that this winds up in the digestive system, causing nausea and upset stomachs. Also, when the body is in a heightened state of alert for prolonged periods of time this can cause stress on the heart and increase one's blood pressure, which causes headaches and muscle aches. And because of being consistently distracted with one's depression and condition, this can cause someone to become clumsy and uncoordinated.

GETTING AN ACCURATE DIAGNOSIS

It is vitally important that anyone that has any of these symptoms to any degree get an accurate diagnosis from a licensed healthcare professional.

Depression is one of the most misdiagnosed illnesses and one that is often overlooked. Rarely does anyone want to admit that they suspect that they suffer from clinical depression, and rarely do doctors make the connection when it comes to physical ailments, mood swings, lack of motivation, and so on. Far too many assume that they are just going through a bad time, need some iron in their blood, or something else that is dismissive.

And at the same time, many of these physical ailments can be caused by any number of other ailments and do not necessarily add up to clinical depression. So it's imperative that you reach an accurate diagnosis.

Clinical depression is an illness or a condition just like how pneumonia or a broken bone is an illness and a condition. It is not a sign of weakness and is not something that can be wished away or conquered just through the strength of your own will. It is not to be confused with "the blues" or a temporary mood that is brought on by a rainy day, a sad movie, or just plain stress. It is also dangerous for the sufferer as he or she may make many mistakes in trying to treat the disease that are just going to make symptoms worse and increase their suffering needlessly.

Depression is also very treatable and even curable. It is possible to learn new ways of thinking and behaving that will help to alleviate the symptoms and there are many new treatment options available that can keep those symptoms at bay.

WHAT CAUSES DEPRESSION

There is probably no subject in the world more complex than that of human emotion. Even after thousands of years of human history, it seems that people are no closer to explaining what they feel and why they feel that way than the cavemen were. Ask a man what he's feeling and you'll get a blank stare; ask a woman about her feelings and you'll need to get comfortable.

Human emotion is a complex issue because while it's often caused by outside factors - you feel upset because you lost a job, you feel angry because traffic was miserable - those factors simply trigger a chain of events that happen inside. In other words, traffic itself isn't making you miserable, but the traffic and the way you feel about it sets off certain chemical reactions in your brain that in turn cause you to feel frustrated, angry, irritated, and so on.

One of the reasons that human emotions are such a difficult subject to discuss and in turn treat is that they are as different for each individual as their own fingerprint. Two people driving in that same traffic jam are going to have two different reactions to it - one gets overly irritated, while another hardly notices the imposition.

It's important to understand this when talking about what causes depression because far too often people think that they should just be able to take a pill and presto, their depression is gone. While medication may work for some and in varying degrees for others, it's extremely shortsighted to assume that depression can be so easily treated and cured in anyone.

Let's take a closer look at what is derived as typical causes for clinical depression in most people so that you have a better understanding of why this condition is so unique to everyone and can make better decisions about its treatment.

ASSUMPTION 1: THE BODY'S CHEMICALS AND HORMONES

Our moods are caused and controlled by chemicals and hormones in the brain; when we enjoy a good movie or a good joke, laughing causes a release of dopamine, or the "feel good" chemical in the brain, which in turn makes us feel good and enjoy the laughter. Eating also releases this chemical, which is why some turn to food for comfort. There are many other things that we do that can trigger the release of these positive chemicals and hormones, such as exercise, take illicit drugs, get a good night's sleep, and so on.

As the body has positive hormones and chemicals that make us feel good, it also had negative chemicals and hormones that make us feel stressed or anxious. At first glance we may think that the body has no use for these negative emotions but remember to look at the big picture. When we feel afraid we tailor our actions accordingly and may therefore protect ourselves - we're fearful of that slippery road we're driving on, so we slow down. We hear a noise in our home at night and become afraid so we grab something to protect ourselves or call the police. That fear leads to positive action that is beneficial.

Our emotions are all either designed to bring about action that protects us or in some way connects us socially. Anger is typically thought to bring about the "fight or flight" reaction, where we are either readying to fight an opponent or are ready to flee. We feel grief because death is something that tears at those social fabrics.

Realizing how the body's physical makeup is affected by outside influences helps us to understand some different ways that depression can be caused by certain circumstances.

ASSUMPTION 2: GENETICS

It's also believed that depression seems to run in families, so there must be some type of genetic predisposition to the condition as well as having it caused by outside influences. Bear in mind too that any part of the body and any part of its composition can be defective or unbalanced; people can be born with all sorts of allergies and sensitivities to food and other seemingly harmless items, so if you can be born with allergies certainly it seems that you can be born with chemical imbalances in the brain.

Note what WebMD states about the physical roots of those with depression:

"There is absolute proof that people suffering from depression have changes in their brains compared to people who do not suffer from depression. The hippocampus, a small part of the brain that is vital to the storage of memories, is smaller in people with a history of depression than in those who've never been depressed. A smaller hippocampus has fewer serotonin receptors. Serotonin is a neurotransmitter -- a chemical messenger that allows communication between nerves in the brain and the body.

What scientists don't yet know is why the hippocampus is smaller. Investigators have found that cortisol (a stress hormone that is important to the normal function of the hippocampus) is produced in excess in depressed people. They believe that cortisol has a toxic or poisonous effect on the hippocampus. It's also possible that depressed people are simply born with a smaller hippocampus and are therefore inclined to suffer from depression."[1]

It is generally believed that some are genetically predisposed to it, others have it thrust upon them because of various circumstances.

ASSUMPTION 3: OUTSIDE CIRCUMSTANCES

Negative emotions can of course stay with us for a long period of time, even after the circumstances causing them are gone. You have a bad day at work and you continue to be in a bad mood even after you've gotten home; you and your mate are having problems and you seem to be perpetually upset and irritated even when you're at work or aren't with him or her.

Scientists and doctors are still trying to figure out why we have these lingering feelings even after the outside circumstances have passed. The sufferings of post- traumatic stress disorder are hard to understand and even more difficult to treat. Someone that was in a bad or traumatizing situation can suffer from stress, anger, anxiety, and constant fear for years after the situation is over. A person that was abused as a child can have feelings of disgust, anger, frustration and guilt well into their adult years.

Even though doctors are still unsure of how and why this happens, and are even further away from a solution, the point is that there are circumstances that can happen that cause us to have negative emotions for years and years. It's believed that depression can be caused by outside circumstances that continue to cause a person to be suffering from this condition even after this particular circumstance is over.

Here are some common examples of outside reasons why someone would be more likely to experience depression:

Child abuse, whether physical, sexual, mental or emotional.

Childhood trauma, such as the loss of a parent at an early age.

Prolonged illness or serious injury.

Traumatic events such as a serious car accident, natural disaster, or crime.

Being in an abusive marriage or other such relationship.

Major events such as changing or losing a job (this includes retirement), moving to a new neighborhood, divorce, children moving out of the house, or graduating.

Isolation from family or loss of friends. For example, some who reveal that they are homosexual or that they are romantically involved with someone their family disapproves of are then cast off from that social circle, leading to depression. This can also happen to those with mental illnesses, who are experiencing financial problems, who change religions, or for any other reason they are now ostracized from those they were once close to.

Prolonged grief from sudden or unexpected deaths, such as that of a child or sibling.

Witnessing a horrific event, such as a car accident or physical assault. While it's unclear why these circumstances will cause a person to become depressed and stay depressed long after they have passed, the most popular theory is that when someone goes through or witnesses such horrific things, the brain's chemistry becomes so upset that it cannot go back to normal. You might compare this to someone that becomes severely overweight for any length of time; their metabolism becomes very skewed so that it's not easily corrected.

OTHER CAUSES OF DEPRESSION

There are other causes of depression, including:

Substance abuse; this includes prescription medications, over-the- counter medications, and alcohol abuse.

Childbirth.

Some medications.

Head trauma or injury.

Social isolation.

Prolonged stress.

Other mental and emotional illnesses, such as panic attacks, phobias, Obsessive Compulsive Disorder, and the like. It's believed that some of these cause depression because they interfere with the body's normal chemical balances and functions, such as when a person abuses any type of drugs or medications. Other situations such as stress and illness can bring about a sense of hopelessness and suicidal thoughts as a person feels as if their situation will just never improve, or that so much damage has been done to them and their life that they will never recover completely.

THE MAIN CAUSE FOR DEPRESSION

Outside circumstances can trigger a depressive episode or chronic clinical depression in some people, but bear in mind that the exact same circumstances may not affect someone else in the same way. Anyone that goes through an abusive childhood or traumatic event is going to suffer some negative emotions, but it's apparent that some people suffer negatively more than others. While some people continue to be depressed for a lifetime, others seem to be able to move on from such events and are able to return to a healthy emotional state.

The reason that it's important to realize this is because people are often able to pinpoint the circumstance that has triggered their depression, but then wonder why it's caused their depression and why the depression hasn't lifted now that they're no longer in that situation.

These circumstances and situations may trigger clinical depression in someone, but obviously there needs to be something about that person that causes them to react that way rather than to "bounce back" or to recover the way someone else will.

Also, some people will change certain circumstances they assume may be causing their depression but then find that they just don't feel better. They may change jobs, get married, get divorced, have children, give away all their possessions, do volunteer work, and so many other things but just don't seem to feel any better.

It's also important to realize that depression is something that is happening internally because someone may begin to blame other people for their condition, whether innocently or maliciously. Since they no longer feel any joy in being a parent, they blame their children or mate for making them feel bad.

Or since they no longer enjoy their job, they assume that the job itself is causing the depression in the first place.

While it's important to address any circumstances that are upsetting or negative such as an abusive relationship or dead-end job, it's also important to realize that sometimes a change of scenery is not enough to "cure" clinical depression and that it's usually not the fault of one's family, friends, coworkers, or anyone else.

DIFFERENT FORMS OF DEPRESSION

There is virtually no type of illness that a person can have that manifests itself in any one particular way. When you have a cold, it could be a head cold, chest cold, or upper respiratory infection. It might affect your sinuses and make you feel achy all over - or not. Because everyone's physical and chemical makeup is different, illnesses will affect each person in a unique and special way unlike how it will affect anyone else.

With clinical depression, the actual illness will affect each sufferer in a unique and different way and of course each patient will experience different levels of severity with it as well. Some will have depression that makes them feel miserable every day but will still manage to get to work whereas others become so low and so full of self-loathing that they wind up becoming suicidal.

It's also true that there are different forms of depression that doctors have managed to pinpoint and classify and that seem to be common to many. Let's explore those different types of depression here.

POSTPARTUM DEPRESSION

"Postpartum" refers to after childbirth. In recent years doctors were discovering that many new mothers were reporting feelings of sadness, emptiness, pointlessness, worthlessness, and depression after the birth of their children, something that could not be blamed on physical fatigue and that was to such a noticeable extent that the medical profession could not ignore it.

Postpartum depression became a popular news item many years ago when U.S. movie actor Tom Cruise declared that women needed to treat their postpartum depression with "vitamins and exercise," a claim that was vehemently denied by doctors, biologists, and mothers as well, many of which were exercising regularly and taking care of themselves but that were still experiencing severe forms of depression.

Causes of postpartum depression.

Being overly tired will make anyone feel sad and lethargic, and of course new mothers are very prone to fatigue. Even if they are able to take naps during the day, being awakened many times during the night for regular feedings interrupts one's sleep cycle and makes you feel tired no matter how much you try to "catch up" on your sleep.

Many women work themselves up into such a frenzy when they're expecting that it's only natural to have some feelings of being let down when you return home. Most expect that they'll just be overwhelmed with love and be constantly enthralled with the new baby, or take their expectations even further than that - thinking the child will solve their marital problems, make them feel loved and worthwhile, and so on. When expectations are this unrealistic it's no wonder that a new mother can feel somewhat disappointed and perhaps a little sad when she's at home with a newborn.

Additionally because a woman is experiencing a severe flux of hormones during pregnancy and after, it's no wonder that she would have mood swings and strong emotional reactions to everyday occurrences. Estrogen is produced in record levels during and after pregnancy, and may bring about mood swings and irritability much like premenstrual syndrome.

The thyroid gland may also be affected by pregnancy and childbirth. The thyroid regulates metabolism and a lower metabolism leads to tiredness and fatigue, lethargy, and a lack of motivation for even everyday actions.

A new mother may still be in a tremendous amount of physical pain as well, which in turn can lead to feelings of depression and sadness or irritability.

Other causes of depressed feelings after childbirth can include:

Grief over perceived loss - the loss of your freedom, your youth, your figure, your friendships with single friends, your status as the only woman in the house, and so on. While some of these losses may be very real others may just be perceived losses in the new mother's mind, although her feelings are very real nonetheless.

Feelings of "cabin fever;" this can be especially true for a mother that was very active or that worked outside the home before becoming pregnant, who now resents or dislikes the time she must spend indoors and somewhat isolated from others.

Overwhelming expectations from others. When friends and family visit often during the first few days and weeks after a new baby, a mother can feel overwhelmed with people and with their expectations, or even her own. It's difficult enough to deal with the new baby and all of his or her demands, and to deal with a lack of sleep and physical pain, but new mother's then feel obligated to keep their house clean for company, to play hostess, and to act as if she's "superwoman" or she'll be looked down on by others. Again, some of these expectations and thoughts may be valid while others are simply in the new mother's own mind, but they still add to her depressed feelings. Real postpartum depression. While most of these conditions and attitudes can be called the "baby blues," or are just typically emotions experienced after childbirth, true postpartum depression is much more severe than any of these conditions. The baby blues typically subside after some time or are just an annoyance that simply need to be dealt with as part of one's everyday life. However, postpartum depression is much worse than this. When a new mother suffers from true postpartum depression, her feelings interfere with her everyday life to the point where she feels no interest in the baby or herself, or with anything else about her daily life. She may have crying jags that last for days or may feel sad enough that she thinks of hurting herself. Other symptoms of true postpartum depression include:

Loss of appetite that can't be attributed to being too busy to cook or eat, or to the physical pain one still feels after childbirth.

Overwhelming feelings of guilt.

Restlessness, anxiety, or loneliness that doesn't subside or that is to extreme extents.

Sudden and extreme mood swings.

Fear of harming the baby. Postpartum psychosis. Psychosis is a severe form of any mental disorder that is characterized by a separation from reality, where the sufferer may have hallucinations, delusions, or uncontrolled thoughts. Psychosis usually happens with those that have schizophrenia or a paranoid type of mental illness. Approximately 1 out of every 1000 new mothers will experience postpartum depression to the point of postpartum psychosis; typically this occurs in women who were already experiencing mental illnesses or who have a predisposition to it. With postpartum psychosis, a mother experience delusions, hallucinations, extreme sleep disturbances, and obsessive thoughts about the baby or herself. She may also experience rapid and extreme mood swings, from suicidal thoughts to feelings of euphoria.

MAJOR DEPRESSIVE DISORDER

The most extreme form of depression is referred to as major depressive disorder. This is for those who suffer from depression to the point where they can barely function on a daily basis, if they can function at all. They seem to drag around every moment with the weight of the world on their shoulders and withdraw from social and everyday activities, including their own career, family, friends, and necessary chores (grocery shopping, cleaning, paying bills); some even neglect their own hygiene and personal care. Many also lose their appetite or go on eating binges, lack interest in sexual activity, and often sleep for hours on end. Those with major depressive disorder are the ones most likely to be suicidal or to harm themselves. They feel hopeless and also feel as if their situation will never change; they see no light at end of the tunnel, so to speak.

ATYPICAL DEPRESSION

Atypical depression is marked by the same symptoms of major depressive disorder but at the same time, the sufferer can sometimes feel moments of elation and even euphoria. Those with atypical depression usually believe that outside forces are influencing their mood, whether it's positive (praise, attention, success) or negative (criticism, failure).

Those with atypical depression usually also experience weight gain and eating disorders as well.

PSYCHOTIC DEPRESSION

Those with psychosis of any type see and hear things that are not real, such as voices talking to them, figures hiding behind trees, and so on. Those with schizophrenia also typically see and hear hallucinations, but those with psychotic depression have these hallucinations in conjunction with their depressive disorder. The depression is bringing on their hallucinations, or vice versa.

DYSTHYMIA

Sometimes a person's mood or feelings are just part of their personality; some people are very happy all the time and love to laugh and make jokes, while others are just naturally more serious or studious. Those with dysthymia seem to have depression and depressed feelings as just part of their personality. They have been sad and melancholy all their lives and have always felt unimportant, dissatisfied, frightened, and just lacking joy in their lives.

Dysthymia is a type of depression but may also be something caused by one's early experiences in childhood. Sometimes sadness can be a learned behavior if one's parents were very stoic and pessimistic. A person can learn to react to life's events by always finding the negative or by cutting themselves down even if they're experiencing some success or other positives. By the same token, there does seem to be some genetic and physical factors involved as well, since medication typically helps these ones as well.

MANIC DEPRESSION

Manic depression or bipolar disorder is characterized by mood swings from depressed and suicidal to ones of extreme euphoria and elation. Both specters of the mood swings are to extreme degrees; this is not to be confused with mood swings that everyone feels from time to time or with those experienced by women with an influx of hormones. When someone suffering from manic depression is at their low point they are often suicidal and go through other motions of harming themselves, and when their mood is at an upswing they may go for days without sleeping, may engage in bizarre behavior such as repainting the home in the middle of the night, and may have delusions or grandeur or a sense of invincibility.

Those with manic depression are prone to suicide more so than other depression patients and need to be under a doctor's supervised care as much as possible. Even during their mood upswings can they be a danger as they may engage in dangerous behavior while disregarding the consequences.

OTHER TYPES OF DEPRESSION

As said, not everyone has any illness in exactly the same way as anyone else. There are different severities of each type of depression, and some types that don't seem to fit into a preconceived mold.

Other types of depression that don't fit the above categories include:

Adjustment or reactive depression where one suffers negative thoughts and feelings after a major life change such as a move, graduation, retirement, and so on. While most people experience a range of emotions after such a life change and these emotions may include sadness or a feeling of grief, when these feelings are severe enough to interfere with one's everyday activities and last longer than six months or so, they can be categorized as depression.

Depression, not otherwise specified. This category includes anyone that does not fit any of these categories but is still suffering from depression in one form or another.

HOW DEPRESSION AFFECTS THE SUFFERER AND THOSE AROUND HIM OR HER

Depression is just an inconvenience, right? Just an annoyance that the sufferer should learn to manage and get over, right?

Those who suffer from clinical depression and those around the sufferer would no doubt beg to disagree. True clinical depression is more than just a minor annoyance or sour mood; it's something that can affect a person's career, every single interpersonal relationship they have, and even threaten their own life.

It's unfortunate that those who have depression are often so wrapped up in or are so overwhelmed by their condition that they rarely give thought to how it is affecting others. Or they may be keenly aware of how their condition is affecting their interpersonal relationships and may know that their family is being neglected and their career is suffering, but without the necessary tools to fix or address their situation they are at a loss as to how to correct this.

Here are some common ways that depression affects the sufferer and those around him or her. Read through these carefully and see if you haven't noticed some of these circumstances in your own life.

LOSS OF INTEREST

A loss of interest seems to be the one common denominator in most cases of depression. Not only are sufferers not interested in developing new hobbies or in setting and reaching new goals for themselves, they are also typically not interested in the things that once brought them happiness. This includes their former hobbies, their families, and even sexual activity.

In addition, this loss of interest extends to their everyday chores and responsibilities so that they may neglect their family, their home, and even themselves.

How this affects others.

Chances are that very few of us actually enjoy every little chore and responsibility we have around the home and at our jobs. We don't necessarily enjoy paying bills and balancing the checkbook or cleaning the bathroom, and don't enjoy the weekly sales meeting with the boss, and so on. But usually we muster up the strength to get through these things and do them anyway simply because we know they need to be done.

For those who are depressed their lack interest and motivation is so overwhelming that they become borderline neglectful of their own family and their career. It's not unusual for children with depressed parents to show up at school without having had breakfast and with no lunch packed or other things they need. Usually children need to become very independent very early on, handling personal chores that are usually beyond them such as their own laundry, own transportation needs to and from school, and so forth.

This loss of interest extends even beyond taking care of children and reaches to a person's home, career, and personal life. Their bills don't get paid on time because they can't make themselves handle that; their home is usually dirty with piles of laundry stacked everywhere.

A person's career, if they have one, also suffers greatly. Usually they take excessive sick time from work and neglect their responsibilities once there. Correspondence goes unanswered and projects are left to the last minute.

And all of this is because the depressed person just cannot find the motivation to be interested in these things. They're just not interested in paying their bills or doing laundry and have a constant "what's the use?" attitude towards everything. Since they see no point in handling personal or career responsibilities, these things are left undone.

This thinking can have a great affect on one's marriage as the loss of interest can mean that a person is now mentally and emotionally absent from their relationship. Their loss of interest can even extend to activities that spouses once enjoyed together, whether that be sports, movies, dancing, and so on. Sexual activity also becomes more of chore than an enjoyment for those that are depressed, also causing great stress on one's relationship.

CONSTANT SADNESS

Have you ever been around someone that seemed to find something wrong with everything, and felt that their bad attitude just seemed to suck the joy out of every activity and every circumstance? Those with depression just cannot find joy in anything, even things that are meant to be joyful.

Most with depression realize how their constant and chronic sadness is sapping the joy from their own life. They no longer look forward to things such as holidays and family dinners, hobbies, and so on. This feeling of sadness extends even when there is no reason to be sad or melancholy.

How this affects others.

For some reason it's difficult to enjoy events or activities if those around us aren't enjoying them. A movie might make you laugh but if the person you're with is crying, you lose a lot of your own enjoyment.

This type of effect can happen for virtually any type of activity or circumstance that a person experiences. Funny movies or television shows are unappreciated, family dinners are no longer fun, and even enjoyable activities can not only bring no happiness to a depressed person, they can even trigger a crying jag or make the depressed mood even worse.

People around a depressed person can pick up on this sadness or at the very least feel as if their own joy is being drained, and of course resentment builds. Some feel as if they deserve to enjoy that family dinner or great movie or just life in general and can get easily irritated at the depressed person.

PHYSICAL MANIFESTATIONS

Persons who are depressed are usually fatigued and lethargic. They often oversleep or spend hours in bed or just reclining on the couch. Rarely do they have the energy to handle just everyday chores, much less the energy to engage in hobbies and other activities.

This can be very difficult for the patient to deal with, as their lack of energy interferes with their everyday activities. They may want to do their housework or take care of their children and their other responsibilities, but they feel as if physically they are buried under a huge weight or burden.

How this affects others.

When a parent spends all day in bed, of course a child suffers. Children need not just attention to their physical needs but their emotional and mental needs as well. Parents who are depressed often cannot muster up the energy to even listen to how their day was, much less can they assist with homework or take them to a friend's house, or allow the child's friends to visit either.

Marriages suffer because one spouse of course is not ready to spend the rest of life in bed with their mate. They want to be involved in activities as a couple but their spouse simply doesn't have the energy to visit friends, go out, or anything else.

In addition, physical fatigue may also mean that one spouse is neglecting certain responsibilities around the house, at work, or in the relationship itself. A husband may come home to find that his wife hasn't done any housework, hasn't prepared a meal, and so on. A wife may find that her depressed husband hides in the bedroom or den at night, sleeping for hours, and is avoiding activities and housework on the weekends. Resentment easily builds in these areas as one spouse may feel as if he or she is handling the responsibilities of two people.

They may reason that depression or fatigue is "no excuse" and expect their spouse to simply handle certain responsibilities and engage in activities regardless of whether or not they have the energy or motivation.

EFFECTS AT THE OFFICE

It's easy to think that one's condition is not the boss' business, and that as long as you show up for work then he or she has no reason to complain. There are some things to think about when it comes to depression's affect on one's career and at the office.

While a person's physical health is typically no business of one's employer, it's important to remember that an employer is paying the patient a salary and should rightly expect a certain amount of work and professionalism in return.

When a boss or manager is consistently disappointed because of deadlines not being met, customer demands being ignored, and just a very poor and pessimistic attitude, you can then understand how depression affects one's employer. While of course this situation is different from someone that is choosing to have a bad attitude or that is just lazy and irresponsible, the bottom line is that one's depression does affect those they work with, their employer, their customers, and so on. As a matter of fact, it's not unusual for those with severe cases of depression to be constantly and chronically unemployed as they often lose what jobs they get.

OTHER'S EMOTIONS

It's easy for a sufferer of depression to think that this situation or condition is their own business and doesn't deserve a reaction from anyone else, but remember that as complex as your emotions are, this is how complex other person's emotional reactions can be as well. Let's examine some common feelings and reactions of those who live with and work with those who have depression.

Resentment and anger.

Being resentful of someone else's illness is not limited to those that are depressed. Family and friends can be resentful of someone in a wheelchair, that is severely obese, or that for some other reason has an illness that interrupts or interferes with their own life or that requires special consideration and help.

It's easy to say that someone shouldn't be resentful or angry of someone else's condition if it's not their fault and there's nothing they've done to bring this on, and this is a true statement. But keep in mind that often feelings like resentment are just natural reactions to situations that are unfair. You are angry when needing to sit in traffic on your way home, even though bad traffic is not necessarily anyone's fault in particular. You resent the rain that falls on your weekends or vacation days, although it's obviously not the fault of anyone around you or anyone in particular. Resentment and anger are just emotions that are complex and difficult to pinpoint and even more difficult to control.

Many who live with those that are depressed suffer from resentment of those patients. They resent the fact that they can no longer enjoy activities that they once did, that responsibilities are not being taken care of, and so on. They are angry that this person cannot just "snap out of it," and may be angry that certain treatment methods do not seem to be working. They may also resent the time and the money spent on one's health care as well.

Guilt.

When someone you love or care about is sad or depressed, of course you want to cheer them up. It's human nature to want to say a few kind words or to give some encouragement so they can put a smile back on their face and move past whatever it is that's depressing them.

When it comes to clinical depression, it's not uncommon for other friends and family members to feel guilty because they can't "fix" the problem. They may try and try to say encouraging things or to remind this person why they have reason to be cheerful, and to no avail.

Children especially seem to be prone to guilt feelings when it comes to a parent with depression. Since the parent takes no interest in their care or their activities, they assume that they are "in the way" or that they are the cause of the depression in the first place.

Guilt often follows the feelings of resentment and anger, as many who live with the sufferers of depression know that they shouldn't feel resentful or angry and so then they feel guilty.

UNDERSTANDING THESE EMOTIONS AND EFFECTS

Simply saying that someone else shouldn't feel angry or resentful or guilty over a person's depression is just as useless as saying that a persons shouldn't feel depressed. You truly can't regulate emotions simply by saying what you should or shouldn't feel

Emotions like anger, resentment or guilt are just as much a part of one's life as the emotions of happiness and joy. Telling someone they "shouldn't" feel angry at something is like saying you shouldn't find a joke funny. Yes, you can work at controlling these emotions and certainly can take responsibility for how the emotions affect one's actions, but expecting that you'll just never feel these emotions at all, ever, simply because you don't think you should is shortsighted.

DEALING WITH GUILT

Feeling guilty can actually be a beneficial thing; that pang of conscience is unpleasant enough to motivate you to avoid doing something wrong next time around. It also shows that we are concerned with how our activities affect other people or shows a sense of responsibility - we feel guilty if we cheat on our taxes, not because it necessarily affects any one particular person but because we feel responsible for paying taxes. The sense of guilt is a good gage for own sense of responsibility.

Guilt is a very interesting emotion however because it is one of those that is most commonly felt when there is no justifiable reason for it. A person can feel tremendously guilty when they haven't done anything wrong.

PINPOINTING YOUR GUILT

If you're plagued with guilt, rather than avoid it try to examine it carefully. What is making you feel guilty? What things come to your mind that make you feel guilty? Is it one particular event or shortcoming you have? Is it the expectations your parents heaped upon you that you just couldn't seem to live up to? Are those expectations now coming from your boss, your spouse, your children, and so on?

Do you just feel guilty in general, perhaps because you're not what you think you should be? You're not thin enough, successful enough, rich enough, you don't keep your house perfectly, you snap at your kids every now and again ... and the list goes on.

It's somewhat painful to think seriously about your guilt but by pinpointing it and its reasons then you can take the necessary steps to fix it.

DEALING WITH GUILT

There are a few things you can ask yourself and tell yourself to have a better understanding of your guilt and of how to get past it and move on to healthier ways of thinking.

If you really have done something wrong that makes you feel guilty, really, how bad was it? Everyone is imperfect, loses their temper, says things they regret, and so on. By mentally beating yourself up, does your punishment really fit the crime? Is it not time to forgive yourself, accept yourself, and move on?

If your guilt is coming from your parents' expectations or from a demanding boss or spouse that you can never seem to please, you need separate your own expectations from theirs. If you're an adult, it's time to set aside your parents' thoughts and demands and live your own life. If you have a demanding boss or spouse, keep in mind that just because they criticize you this doesn't mean you have necessarily done anything wrong. Some people are just critical and demanding by nature, especially if they find someone that refuses to stand up to them.

When you feel guilty for your life in general, it's time to get some balance. What are your priorities, and how can you improve upon reaching those? If other issues are not a priority with you, why be concerned with them? Decide for yourself what is important - family, career, home, health, and so on - and what is not important, and let go of your expectations for the things that aren't important to you. And, be balanced when it comes to the things that are.

OTHER WAYS TO DEAL WITH GUILT

A sense of balance and reasonableness is important to dealing with unnecessary guilt. We often need to put our own behavior and actions in perspective and realize that we're no more imperfect than the next person. Setting goals for improvement also helps.

Sometimes guilt is appropriate if we are perhaps lacking in certain areas or have some things we should be working on. Setting goals for personal improvement is a big help when it comes to dealing with guilt because of these things.

As an example, suppose you feel guilty for having outbursts because of a bad temper. Be determined to work on this by recognizing your triggers that set you off, and learn new ways of dealing with it in a patient manner. If you seem to always snap at your children, realize that children are always underfoot; that's just part of being a child. Don't take your irritation out on them, and be prepared to walk away for a few moments before you speak to them.

As you work to improve yourself in any way, your guilt for old mistakes can be lessened.

DEALING WITH A LACK OF SELF-ESTEEM

A lack of self-esteem or feelings of worthlessness seem to be very common to those suffering from clinical depression. If you feel that much of your depression comes from a lack of self-esteem, what can you do to deal with it?

RECOGNIZE YOUR OWN THOUGHTS

It's interesting how two people can be in very similar situations but feel very different about those situations. Two people can have very obnoxious bosses and one will feel terrible every day while the other just shrugs it off.

This is because while other people certainly can make you feel bad about yourself, you can also decide not to let them affect you needlessly. It is actually your own thoughts that are making you feel bad; either you believe a person's criticisms or you don't.

This type of reasoning is much easier said than done, but once you recognize the difference between what other people think and say and what you're obligated to think yourself, you can then move forward.

DEALING WITH IT

Building up self-esteem is a very difficult process, especially if your self-esteem has been chipped away at for years. If your parents abused you for twenty years, you may need another twenty years to fix the problem; nothing gets done overnight.

But building up self-esteem is like losing weight - if you make a plan and stick with it, you'll get small results right away and then even more results down the road.

Your first step is to really think about your priorities and what it is that you think is important in life and as goals and values for a person, and then contrast this to the thoughts that are eroding your self-esteem.

As an example, suppose you place a high value on a person being responsible about working and paying their own bills, but you don't really value a materialistic lifestyle. Being responsible enough to have a job is important to you, but being a big-shot manager or business owner driving a fancy car and having all sorts of money isn't important. But you feel bad about yourself because your job isn't fancy or necessarily important or bringing in six figures. By your own admission, you are actually living a life that's important and valuable to you - you work, pay your bills, and are responsible. And yet you let someone else's values chip away at your self-esteem! Someone else is judging you or degrading you because your job is not that prominent, but you still have the things that are important to you.

As an exercise to do this, tick off all the items below that you personally find important or value. Remember, this is what you think is important, not what your parents told you was important or what your spouse thinks or anyone else.

Important	Not Important	
		Having a job, regardless of what it is or what it pays; hard work and responsibility.
		Having an important or prestigious career; validation from colleagues, superiors, etc.
		Having large sums of money, whether from your paycheck every week or in the bank as savings.
		Having the best of material things.
		Having Children
		Being an involved parent for your children.
		Freedom from the rat race; time to yourself, being in control of your own schedule.

Important	Not Important	
		Lots of friends and a wide social circle and active social life.
		Religious pursuits and involvement.
		Political work and involvement.
		Charity work.
		Schooling, learning, continuing one's education whether for your career for just for the sake of knowledge itself.
		Personality traits that include being polite, modest, and just generally nice to people.

Now that you've gone through this list, add some of your own thoughts and opinions here. What other things do you value and that are important to you as a person? Is it the approval of your friends or your parents? Whatever it is that's important to you, write it in here:

JUDGING BY YOUR OWN STANDARDS

If you look over this list you might begin to realize that you lack of self-esteem is not because you don't have the things that you value, but because you don't feel as if you're living up to someone else's standards.

Some however might immediately begin arguing and saying that it is their own standards to which they are not measuring up. You may value good personality traits but feel as if your temper is making you an undesirable person, or you value being an involved parent but realize that you're just not as good of a parent as you think you should be.

The first thing you need to do, once you've determined what your own values are and recognize your own shortcoming, is to develop some patience with yourself in these areas. View them as simply areas at which you need to work. And rather than getting overwhelmed with this prospect, make a plan you can work on slowly.

Again using the idea of losing weight, no one is going to drop a hundred pounds in a month; it's just not possible or physically healthy. But someone that draws up a healthy eating plan for themselves, and that then works at it a little bit every day is going to find that he or she can lose a pound this week, a pound next week, and so on until they are finally at their goal.

So what can you do today, this week, to improve your situation?

Remember too that sometimes just working on your situation is enough to replenish your self-esteem. You don't need to be at your goal to value yourself or to be proud. If you just start working at it, you'll find it gives you the assurance that you are indeed a valuable and worthwhile person.

DEALING WITH "ALL OR NOTHING" THINKING

One of the most common ways of thinking that many depressed persons have can be referred to as "all or nothing" or perfectionism. Someone thinks that if they can't be perfect and do everything perfectly, then there's no point in doing anything at all. This drive and pressure is overwhelming but unhealthy and imbalanced.

DOES THIS AFFECT YOU

You may immediately recognize this symptom in yourself as you try to go about your day. However, ask yourself these questions:

Do you often give yourself a mental "beating" because of how you've done anything, including even the most mundane of tasks?

Do you often think that you're not good enough even when it comes to things you should enjoy, such as your hobbies or sports?

Are you often plagued by feelings of guilt and frustration when you receive even the slightest criticism, or don't get the praise you thought you would? Perfectionism or the "all or nothing" thinking can be something that you learned in childhood from a very demanding parent, or can be something you bring upon yourself. Wanting praise and reinforcement is of course natural but imposing unhealthy and unbalanced standards upon yourself is not going to accomplish anything.

HOW TO GET PAST IT

Getting past your own perfectionism is a very difficult task but is something that needs to be done. In order to get past it, you first need to acknowledge that you're doing this to yourself. Often those with perfectionist thoughts have this so engrained in their thinking that they rarely even see it as being unhealthy and unbalanced. But once you realize that you have unrealistic expectations for yourself, consider the following:

Ask yourself whose standards are being violated if your home is not spotlessly clean, if you turn in a report at work that is not "perfect," or if you don't bowl a perfect game, play the piano perfectly, and so on. You may think that other people will look down on you if you're not faultless, but once you think about it you may realize that these standards are coming from within.

Once you realize that you are setting these standards for yourself, it's then time to start talking back to yourself. Why do you think your house is too dirty, or your work not good enough or that you're not a good bowler, and so on? Why do you need your boss to lavish praise on you to think you're a good worker, or that you need your mother's approval at the age that you're at?

Really, who is perfect? It's so easy to think that everyone else has their life in order and of course there will always be people that are better than you at something - a better housekeeper, a better lawyer, a better bowler, and so on - but no one is perfect. The people you work with and live next door to also have their imperfections and foibles and areas they need to work at. The woman in the next cubicle might keep a nicer home but you may be more organized; your friend from college may be more successful in his career than you are, but maybe you have a better sense of humor.

If you do have a tendency to suffer from perfectionism because you compare yourself to others, why are you keeping score? What does that person's life has to do with yours? If your friend from college is more successful, so what? That doesn't take away from your success at all, does it? If that woman in the next cubicle is a better housekeeper, that doesn't take away from the hard work you do for your family, does it?

WHAT TO DO

When you have unhealthy thoughts that are contributing to your depression, you need to replace those thoughts with more positive ones. Simply recognizing where those thoughts are coming from is only half the battle.

Some positive thoughts you need to repeat to yourself include:

Being healthy means being balanced. There is no such thing as perfection in this world and you are not going to be the exception to this rule.

Just because you are imperfect does not mean that you are going to lose the love and approval of your friends, family, or workmates. They are imperfect just like you.

Remind yourself of your priorities. Your house may not be in perfect shape but are you spending enough time with your children and your spouse? You may not be a perfect bowler but are you having fun with your friends? Again, this takes a lot of work and effort to replace perfectionist thinking with more balanced thinking, but it can be done.

DEALING WITH HOPELESS THINKING

Someone going through a difficult time period may very well begin to think that things are hopeless, especially if the circumstance seems to drag on endlessly. For example, someone facing chronic employment may begin to wonder if he or she will ever work again; those in bad relationships may assume that they are going to be stuck forever.

As with the perfectionism, hopeless thinking can be very difficult to break away from but it can be done.

DOES THIS AFFECT YOU

Think seriously about the situations in your life that seem to depress you or that add to your depression. This might include poor relationships with your parents, your mate, your children, and so on, or being in a job that you don't care for or that is very stressful, or chronic unemployment or financial problems, or anything else. Take an honest evaluation of your attitudes toward this situation and ask yourself if you have started to think of it as hopeless. Do you feel trapped or stuck, or envision the next twenty or thirty years being in the same situation?

Have these feelings or thoughts kept you from making changes or from dealing with the situation head-on? Do you feel paralyzed by these thoughts or by your feelings of hopelessness?

HOW TO GET PAST IT

Feeling as if a particular situation is hopeless is common for many people and for certain situations. We all occasionally get the thought in our heads that things will just never change, that we're stuck in our bad marriage or bad job or whatever it is.

But when hopelessness becomes to set in and to such an extent that we become severely depressed or refuse to try to make changes, then we need to face this head on.

Ask yourself:

What are the chances that you will never really work again? Even if it takes a year or two years to get another job, so be it. Chances are you won't go your entire life without work.

Are you really stuck in your bad marriage or with poor relations with other family members? Might your spouse also be going through a bad patch, or might your teenagers one day grow up and be mature enough to realize their behavior needs to change?

If your finances or other outside circumstances are giving you grief, remember that you might need many years to fix these things but might patience be in order, rather than giving in to hopelessness?

WHAT TO DO

Substituting healthier thinking for hopeless thoughts is not easy but can be done with patience and determination. You may also need to enlist the aid of friends and family; tell them how you feel and ask them to give you some encouragement and to help you think in a healthier way. They may have some better insights as to your situation and may offer a more balanced point of view. You also need to be determined to really listen to those that give you healthier and more balanced ways of thinking when it comes to hopelessness. It's so tempting to defend one's own unhealthy way of thinking and to shut out our friends and family when they reassure us that things will get better, but in order to get better from depression one must be willing to change one's own thinking.

It might also help to actually write down better thoughts about helplessness and say them out loud. Keep that writing with you at all times and when you hear yourself saying something pessimistic or helpless, take out your list of better thoughts and repeat them out loud.

ASK FOR HELP

Hopeless thinking is one area in which many people should be asking for help, and even more than that, accepting it once it's offered.

If your friends and family know that you are often prone to hopeless thinking, they can come in handy to remind you that things are never hopeless. Yes, situations can be difficult to deal with and it's very discouraging when you are unemployed or having marriage problems and so on, but there's a difference between difficult and hopelessness.

Your friends can be the ones to remind you of that and help you put things in perspective, but you need to willing to listen to what they say and change your own thinking when they do help.

DEALING WITH PERSISTENT SADNESS

Everyone feels sad at one time or another; sadness is part of the difficult world we live in. Simply feeling sad is not some kind of sin within itself and certainly doesn't belie some type of weakness in one's mental state or personality overall.

Sadness can come on for very legitimate reasons such as the loss of a person, loss of a job, loss of freedom, and so on, or may be for reasons that are simulated such as when we cry over a sad movie or TV show.

For persons with depression, sadness seems to be as present as the air they breathe. No matter what you're doing or seeing or who you're with and where you're at, you're sad. This includes even being places or doing things that should make you happy, such as a family dinner, a holiday celebration, a concert or movie, and so on. Nothing cheers you up, nothing makes you happy, nothing can break through that wall of sadness.

DOES THIS AFFECT YOU

This may be obvious; do you feel sad all the time? Does this include times when you shouldn't feel sad, or when everyone else around you is happy? Do you fail to see the joy and amusement in things that should be making you happy, such as a good movie or concert or something else?

Are you sad for no reason; do you just seem to wake up sad and ready to cry? Could you actually sit down and cry at any time? Have you had crying jags or bouts for no reason? Wondering if persistent sadness affects you is not a difficult question, and for most with depression, this is an emotion that's present almost constantly.

HOW TO GET PAST IT

You first need to realize that your sadness is part of your illness and is caused by that imbalance of hormones and chemicals in the brain. Typically these chemicals are sent into overdrive by what we might call legitimate reasons; our pet dies, and we feel sad. We hear of a problem a friend has, and we feel sad. But with chemical depression there's no outside circumstances we need to go through to tip off those chemicals.

You then need to be determined to fight your sadness as you would anything else. Too often we think that if we feel sad, then we're just sad and that's the end of it. But feelings of sadness can be dealt with and changed if one is determined to do just that.

And you need to be determined to let yourself feel happiness again. To many that have clinical depression, happiness is as foreign as a creature from another planet. They don't remember how to be happy and sometimes feel guilty when they do.

WHAT TO DO

It might sound strange to say that you need to work at being happy as most people assume that happiness should just occur, but if you realize that you're sad for no reason and at inappropriate times, you can work at building up your happiness.

First, think about your feelings of sadness. Are they really justified? You may think they are because you've lost someone in death or are dealing with difficult circumstances, but are you just holding on to your negative thinking long past the amount of time you should? Are you holding onto your grief over a loss or anger over some injustice well past a time when it's healthy to do so?

When you realize that your feelings of sadness really are not justified you can then begin to start working on dismissing or ignoring them. When you start to feel the sadness creeping up on you, take decisive action to tell yourself that you just won't entertain those thoughts. Refuse to let yourself give in to those feelings.

The old adage that you need to count your blessing may seem passé but is very appropriate. Think seriously about what things can make you happy, whether that's your children, your family, your work, your self-respect, your hobbies, or anything else.

Concentrate on the positive aspects of these things. Don't allow place for the sadness and instead crowd out those sad feelings with the more positive ones you create for yourself.

Sometimes those with clinical depression need permission from themselves to feel happiness. It's as if they shouldn't be feeling happiness, and this too is a thought that needs to be fought against. You deserve happiness just as much as anyone else, so be sure to tell yourself that constantly.

DEALING WITH A LACK OF INTEREST

Note which of these things no longer hold interest for you even though they once perhaps did:

Your children's activities, including their schoolwork, extracurricular activities, friends, and hobbies.

Hobbies you once enjoyed, including sports activities, movies, music, sewing, scrapbooks, quilting, artwork, reading, and so on.

Activities with your spouse or mate, including shared hobbies and interests, and even sexual activity.

Your work and career.

Your own schooling and intellectual activities, even if this means just having watched PBS once a month or having read a certain magazine every now and again.

Friends and being with them.

Holidays, family reunions, anniversaries, birthdays, and special occasions such as this.

Religious pursuits and activities.

Taking care of your home, your car, and other possessions.

Taking care of yourself, from exercising to even your own personal hygiene. If you checked off even one of these items, you may realize how your lack of interest has affected your functioning in your home and your own life. So let's look at how you can get past your lack of motivation to actually do the things you want to do and know you have to do.

Step One:

Make a list of all the things that you know you're not doing because of your lack of interest. This might include not helping your child with his or her homework, not visiting your family as often as you would like, or not participating in sexual activity enough to make your partner happy. Be very honest with yourself when making this list.

Step Two:

With this list in hand, now make a list of all the things you're missing out by not participating in these activities. You're missing out on some very important bonding time with your children, time with your family and friends, and activities with your spouse. They are not just suffering because of your illness; you are as well.

Consider too all the things that you want to do for yourself that you know you'll enjoy but just don't have the motivation to do, such as exercising, finishing school, and so on. Be generous with this list.

Step Three:

Make a plan for how you'll slowly restart these activities without waiting for the motivation to do so. This is a very important point; you are going to make a plan and stick to it, and nowhere in that plan will it say that once you get motivated then you'll do this or that. You will simply follow through with your plans in spite of your feelings or lack of them.

Here's an example of how this work. Suppose you are missing out on your once weekly dinner at your parents' house because you just don't have any motivation to go. You really just don't have the interest, although you would like to get back to the point when you did enjoy spending time with them. You also realize that your parents are getting older and you don't have time to waste.

So your plan is to choose one weekend day this month when you will go for dinner. You wake up that day and still feel no motivation or concern, as a matter of fact, you'd rather just go back to bed. But your plan is to go, so that's what you're going to do. You don't need to be happy or elated or eager; you're just going, period.

Step Four:

This may seem like an odd step, but it's important to realize that when you have clinical depression and you go through the steps of participating in activities once again, you may not necessarily walk away from them feeling happy and connected as you once did.

It's true that very often people come away from these activities in a better mood and just feeling better than they did before, but forcing yourself into doing certain things or going certain places is not a magic pill that will immediately cure your mood. If you come home from your parents' house or your child's school play or that night class you want to take and still aren't feeling the motivation, don't let that worry you. Usually the better mood and better attitude will come in time, and usually later rather than sooner.

DEPRESSION FREE METHOD: LEARNING NEW THINKING FOR NEW BEHAVIOR

Depression is an illness just as much as a common cold is an illness. You can't talk yourself out of depression any more than you can talk yourself out of having a cold.

However, there is a reason a person gets a cold, and you can take medications that correct the symptoms of your illness and help speed up a cure, or at the very least that can help you feel better enough so that you can function and not be bedridden while ill. In the same way, there are some thoughts or thought patterns that many who have depression seem to fall prey to, and many that can be changed if the person is determined to do just that. This won't cure your depression any more than a sinus pill will cure your cold, but learning new ways of thinking can help keep the negative thoughts you have at bay so that your depression doesn't rule your life.

Let's explain it this way. Pretend that there is someone in your life that you just don't like - for this example, we'll use your mother-in-law. Let's say that you've had some unpleasant confrontations with her in the past and perhaps she has some unpleasant personality traits that just rub you the wrong way. Consequently, every time you see her name on the caller I.D. of a phone call or know it's time to go over to her house for dinner, you just bristle.

These feelings you have for this woman are natural, if you've had unpleasant meetings with her before. However, you can train yourself to start thinking differently about her if you try. You can consider her good points and try to develop some understanding at the same time; is she short-tempered because she has a high pressure job or is in some physical pain? Does she just have a sense of humor that perhaps you find a bit rough whereas others may just see it as homey and down-to-earth? Also, you're imperfect as well and yet you want your friends and family to overlook your own imperfections, so why not do the same for her? While you may never be good friends with your MIL, you may learn some more positive ways of thinking, and therefore feeling, when you are with her or do need to speak with her. This way your negative thoughts about her won't override your activities and detract from your enjoyment while with her.

The same can happen with your depression. You may never be able to talk yourself into not being depressed, but you can certainly learn healthier ways of thinking about your situation and about life in general, and train yourself to concentrate on that thinking rather than allowing your depression to run unchecked. The depression will no doubt still be there, much the same way that your negative feelings about your MIL may always be present, but thoughts do not need to be left uncontrolled, whether that's the thoughts about your MIL or the negative thoughts that are present with depression.

DON'T WAIT FOR MOTIVATION

Why do we do anything that we do? Many of our actions are based on a survival mechanism of course. We eat and sleep because if we didn't our bodies would shut down or otherwise demand that we do through pain or discomfort. We also do many other things because we have the proper motivation to do so. We go to work because we need money to buy food, clothing and shelter, and because it gives us a sense of self-respect and satisfaction. We marry because we're in love and we want companionship. And the list goes on from there.

Motivation comes into play even for things we may not typically want to do. We clean our house, not because we enjoy scrubbing toilets or mopping floors, but because we want that result of a clean house. Same with doing laundry, paying bills, raking the yard, and so on. Our motivation may not be the enjoyment we get from the particular activity but the end result is enough to "make" us take care of that responsibility anyway.

But for a person who suffers from depression, that motivation to do just about anything and everything is gone. There is just no reason, no drive to get out of bed. There is no joy in work or family so we have no reason to take care of our projects or give attention to our children or mate; there is no joy in hobbies, friends, or even sexual activity so there is no reason to partake in these activities. And since a depressed person now has the "what's the use?" attitude, there is no motivation or reason to take care of unpleasant responsibilities or chores either.

Many years ago, a therapist counseling patients with mental and emotional disorders coined the phrase, "Go through the motions, and the emotions will follow."

His point was that we often wait until we feel motivated to do something before we actually do it. However we most certainly can do the things we need to do even without motivation; as a matter of fact, waiting for that motivation can be a huge mistake as it may never come, especially for the person that's depressed.

This might sound like a difficult undertaking and indeed it is. But waiting for that elusive motivation is probably not going to work for anyone suffering from depression, and some have found that if they do indeed go through those motions, they feel much better about themselves and their situation when they do.

NEGATIVE EMOTIONS

Another hindrance to participating in and enjoying activities a depressed person once did, and in taking care of their responsibilities, can be negative emotions of any type. These emotions might include:

Guilt for some perceived sin, whether real or imagined.

Feelings of worthlessness.

Anxiety.

Fear of the future, of disappointing others, and so on.

Lack of self-esteem; feeling that others are looking down on you or laughing at you.

Sadness or grief, whether over a real event or just a general feeling.

Anger or frustration, especially when over a certain injustice, crime, or other negative circumstance. Looking over this list, it's no wonder a depressed person would be hesitant to engage in activities when the only thing they feel is negative. Being active is typically just a constant reminder of these feelings, whereas hiding in bed or in one's home is a convenient way to avoid these feelings.

What to do.

The first thing you need to do is to understand that negative emotions are what they are; they're a part of life and nothing to be ashamed of or to be feared. Everyone has negative emotions from time to time, so feeling guilty or worthless doesn't mean that you are guilty of something or worthless.

Once you acknowledge that negative emotions are part of your life, you can then learn to get past them rather than letting them control you.

The second thing you need to do is make up your mind that you will participate in your activities despite those emotions. We might go back to our illustration of the common cold - you can either go to work feeling sick or allow yourself to get overwhelmed with the cold so that you spend days in bed without good reason.

Yes, it's true that no one likes to go to work with a cold, but again, your choices are to do the things you know you want to do and know you must do or stay at home, in bed, doing nothing. Thinking that you need to feel great and enthused and happy in order to actually participate in those activities is a mistake, just like thinking that you need to wait until your cold clears up before you ever leave the house again can keep you housebound needlessly.

Here are some additional tips on how to get moving and how to get active even when you are feeling only negative emotions:

Set aside some time when you can actually wallow in those emotions. If you feel like you just want to have a crying jag rather than go into work, tell yourself that you'll get through your workday and then spend an hour after dinner doing whatever you want - even if that means just sitting and crying. Don't allow yourself to indulge in your tears until that time.

Realize that participating in those activities will not magically cure your negative emotions; don't set yourself up for disappointment by thinking you'll "beat the blues" by getting active again. Realize that your goal is just to get active physically, while you work on your negative emotions separately.

Keep other people and their interests and well-being in mind as well. If you stay away from your child's school activities, how will that affect him or her? If you don't participate in any activities with your spouse, how will that make him or her feel? By remembering that there are other people that are affected by your actions (or lack of them) you may then be more motivated to go through the motions even if your emotions are not there.

Remember that you will not be automatically happy and excited about participating in activities, but don't let this stop you. If you go through the motions you may find that the joy will eventually return.

MEDICATIONS EXPLAINED IN PLAIN ENGLISH

Oh, if only there were some type of "happy pill" we could all take when we're sad or upset or just need a boost. Unfortunately for some, they confuse many drugs with such pills and self-medicate with illegal substances or assume that some a prescription can cure all their ills.

For others, they make the opposite mistake and avoid all medications and treatment options completely, assuming they'll become addicted or fearing side effects.

Others see medications as a sign of weakness, especially when used for mental and emotional illnesses. They often assume that a person should be able to just mentally address a mental illness, or should be in control of their emotions at all times, if they were "strong enough."

Obviously it's a personal decision as to whether or not one should take medications for any reason and those prescribed for depression need to be considered carefully. They of course are not like taking a cough drop or some aspirin, and the risk of abuse and dependency is greater for some of these.

Before you make that decision, let's consider some simple information about them in plain English so that you can better understand what is being recommended to you, and can then make an informed decision either way.

MONOAMINE OXIDASE INHIBITORS (MAOIS)

Monoamine oxidase is a chemical that breaks down neurotransmitters or chemical messengers in the brain that cause a person to feel calm and relaxed, and when these chemicals or neurotransmitters are out of balance a person can suffer from depression. MAOIs work by reducing the amount of monoamine oxidase so that these chemicals are not broken down and are more in balance, causing a person to feel calmer and less anxious.

Precautions to remember.

MAOIs are not always the first choice of medications used because they react strongly with the chemical in certain foods; a person taking MAOIs needs to be very careful about their dietary habits and with how the medication interacts with other medicines.

Side effects of MAOIs include:

Drowsiness and fatigue

Constipation, nausea, diarrhea, upset stomach

Dry mouth

Dizziness and lightheadedness, especially when getting up from sitting or reclining

Low blood pressure

Decreased urine output

Decreased sexual function

Sleep disturbances

Muscle twitching

Weight gain, increased appetite

Blurred vision

Headache

Restlessness, shakiness, trembling, weakness, sweating

TRICYCLIC ANTIDEPRESSANTS (TCAS)

TCAs also affect the levels of these neurotransmitters but they have more side effects than most other drugs and so are not used that often.

Precautions to remember.

TCAs are affect blood sugar levels, so those with diabetes and other sugar problems are not recommended to take them. They also seem to be associated with an increased risk of heart attack.

Side effects of TCAs include:

Drowsiness

Dry mouth

Blurred vision, dizziness, sensitivity to sunlight

Constipation, nausea, urinary retention

Impaired sexual functioning

Increased heart rate

Disorientation or confusion

Headache

Low blood pressure, weakness

Increased appetite and weight gain

SELECTIVE SEROTONIN REUPTAKE INHIBITORS (SSRIS)

These drugs work by altering the amount of a chemical in the brain called serotonin. Serotonin is a what you would call a "feel good" chemical in the brain and is what causes a person to feel calm, happy and relaxed. Serotonin is released during many things we do that make us happy; when we eat, laugh, or enjoy sexual activity, the brain releases serotonin. Many who suffer from clinical depression seem to have a low level of serotonin or the brain is not releasing it the way it should. SSRIs keep the chemicals that prevent serotonin from being released to over-regulate its levels.

Precautions to remember.

SSRIs seem to be the safest of all antidepressant drugs and have fewer side effects and less interaction with other drugs.

Side effects include:

Nausea, diarrhea

Sexual dysfunction

Headache

Nervousness, agitation, restlessness

Rash

Increased sweating

Weight gain

Drowsiness and insomnia

COPING WITH SIDE EFFECTS

The side effects that are common with antidepressants are the main reason that many people stop taking them. No one wants to trade weight gain for feeling better and dealing with sexual dysfunction or chronic headaches can sometimes make one think if the cure isn't worse than the disease. There are some things you can remember about coping with the side effects of your antidepressants. Regular exercise seems to help with the side effects of nausea and upset stomach, as exercise helps with your blood circulation and digestive system. It can also help with any interruptions of your sleep pattern such as drowsiness and insomnia.

Simple fixes such as sucking ice chips and drinking water constantly throughout the day can help with dry mouth. Keep your home and office adequately humid as well. You can also chew sugarless gum or suck on sugarless candies; be sure to brush your teeth regularly and avoid oral hygiene products that contain alcohol as this too can cause dry mouth.

For problems such as blurred vision, talk to your doctor about using eye drops. Avoid eyestrain by having your surroundings well lighted. Take your time focusing and be sure to blink often.

Other problems may be addressed by taking a so-called "drug holiday" where you stop your dose for just one day per week. However, it's imperative that you always stay in touch with your doctor and get his or her approval before stopping or adjusting your dosage in any way.

NATURAL REMEDIES FOR DEPRESSION

There is and probably always will be controversy about the effectiveness of herbs and other natural remedies for depression and mental illnesses. Some treatment options seem to be effective in some circumstances while others seem to have no difference for those participating in laboratory tests.

St. John's Wort

Also known as goat weed or Klamath weed, St. John's wort has been shown to be effective in some circumstances for treating depression and anxiety, and sleep disorders as well.

While St. John's Wort has been shown to be ineffective for major depressive disorders, it does seem to have a calming and uplifting effect for those with minor depressive episodes. However, it does react with other drugs and medications and can dilute the effect of birth control pills, digoxin, and other antidepressants. Anyone taking St. John's wort should alert their doctor when prescribed any other medications in case of interaction.

Side effects of St. John's wort include nausea, anxiety, headache, confusion, dry mouth, dizziness, gastrointestinal symptoms, fatigue, or sexual dysfunction.

Dietary changes.

Some who suffer from minor depressive episodes have found that changing their diet to eliminate wheat, flour, caffeine, sugar, and chocolate have had their moods lifted. This of course is not going to be effective for everyone but if you have a sensitivity or allergy to a certain food, you may find that the symptoms of that sensitivity will be your depressed feelings, the way others may break out in hives or have swelling when they eat something they're allergic to.

If your depression is accompanied by lethargy and a general feeling of fatigue, bloating, stomach irritation, and symptoms like these, try keeping a food diary for two weeks. Eliminate one item such as sugar or wheat for two solid weeks and then see if your symptoms don't improve any.

This may not cure your feelings but if you do have a sensitivity you can find that you get increased energy and less stomach irritation if you cut out these foods.

DEPRESSION FREE METHOD 10-STEP ACTION PLAN TO OVERCOMING YOUR DEPRESSION

Hopefully by now you've already made some changes in your thinking and your behavior that has helped or that will help you deal with and treat your depression. If you find that you still have some work to do, let's consider this 10- step plan.

1. RECOGNIZE THAT IT'S AN ILLNESS.

Depression won't go away on its own and it won't just clear up one day. If you've been ignoring the symptoms or thinking that one day you'll just snap out of it, you're making a mistake. You need to accept what it is and the fact that you need to address it as an illness before the symptoms will get any better.

And by recognizing that it's an illness you can better understand how just simply exercising and taking vitamins is not going to do the trick. These things can help you feel better about yourself in some circumstances, but for true clinical depression it's going to take more than that.

2. BECOME RESPONSIBLE ABOUT ADDRESSING IT AND TREATING IT.

If you live alone on a deserted island and don't need to work and have no family, then of course you can wallow about in your depression all you want. As a matter of fact, you can do whatever you want, whenever you want, wearing whatever you want.

But if you do have a job, family, and other responsibilities, you need to start addressing this situation and this illness for their sakes as well as for yours. While your illness is of course your business, depression is something that can affect all of those around you including your spouse, children, and anyone else in your life. And it can affect them for years - your children can be neglected, your spouse can be left without much of a mate, and so on. Realizing how much your behavior and your emotions touch other people's lives can be good motivation to make changes.

View the treatment of your depression as just being a responsible adult, the way you would want to deal with anything in your life that affects other people.

3. RECOGNIZE YOUR OWN PARTICULAR SYMPTOMS AND PROBLEMS.

As with any other illness, depression will affect each sufferer in different ways. Some have persistent feelings of sadness while others are plagued with low self- esteem. Still others have the chronic "what's the use?" attitude regardless of what they're doing and where they are, and still others have lost all interest in anything and everything.

Addressing your own particular symptoms and condition is the key to actually fixing those problems in the first place. You need to be honest about yourself and your own condition before you can address it properly.

4. MAKE A PLAN.

Realizing what your symptoms are and what needs to be done to fix or deal with them is not going to magically make that happen. As with wanting to lose weight, find a new job, or accomplish anything else, you need to make an actual step-by- step plan for what you're going to do and how you're going to do it.

Use the information you've found in this book to make a schedule for how you're going to address your symptoms. Do you suffer from a lack of self-esteem? What are you going to do today, this week, and this month to help yourself? Do you avoid activities and association with people because of your depression? What will you do this week and this month to reenter your life?

Your plan should be broken down into manageable steps. You're not going to fix anything overnight, and being overwhelmed with your own expectations is just a recipe for disaster.

5. GO THROUGH THE MOTIONS.

Remember what we talked about, that you shouldn't wait until you "want" to go to your mother's house for dinner or until you feel "motivated" to exercise. Don't wait for your emotions to get in line before you take action. When you have your plan of attack in place, that's what you follow.

Think of it this way. People force themselves to do things every day that they don't like to do and really would rather not be doing. Do you honestly think that all those people that show up for work every day really "feel like" being there? If everyone waited until they wanted to do something before they actually did it, everyone would be unemployed and nothing would ever be accomplished in the world, ever.

Remind yourself that it's the same with you, but all the more so since you have depression. Don't wait until you want to do these things, just do them regardless of how you feel and your levels of motivation.

6. BE PATIENT.

You may not start feeling better right away; as a matter of fact, it might take months and years before your mood improves. But as with any other illness, a cure is not always instant and may not happen when you expect it to. When someone tears ligaments in their knee or breaks a hip, physical therapy schedules are made up for a reason - it can take years before they have full mobility again.

Patience means not giving up the minute you have a setback or start feeling as if you should be further along than you are. It means realizing that things won't happen overnight and that you're still going be struggling for sometime.

7. MAKE A LIFETIME COMMITMENT.

We all wish we could wake up tomorrow and no longer have our own particular problems, frustrations, and worries. Those with money problems would love to have their debts paid off right now; those who battle addictions would love to not worry about if they'll be tempted with alcohol or drugs or unhealthy foods.

Dealing with depression is like dealing with any other chronic problem you may have; it's a lifetime commitment and one that may honestly may never be cured. You might not ever wake up and be completely free of your symptoms of depression, but if you learn these coping mechanisms and are determined to apply them you can find that your life is much less interrupted.

It's unfortunate that you or anyone else needs to deal with the problems of depression but it's a fact of life, just like someone with a physical disability needs to accept that this condition will be with them for life as well. Once you accept that fact however you can then realize that you have two choices - let the condition take over and keep you completely paralyzed, or be determined to make the best of your situation and learn ways of coping and dealing with it.

And as you continue to do this you will find that things get much easier over time. Forcing yourself to go to someone's house for dinner or to take an interest in your child's day when you have that "what's the point?" thinking gets easier over time. Talking back to the negative thoughts you have in your head about your own self- worth becomes automatic and less of a chore.

8. ASK FOR HELP.

No one wants to admit that they need help, and even fewer actually want to accept that help once it's offered. But if your friends and family know about your condition, they're in a better position to give needed help.

Part of this help might mean some tough love. When you feel like staying in bed all day or start taking the "what's the use?" attitude, your friends and family are going to need to tell you things that you don't want to hear, such as the fact that this is just the depression talking.

Asking for help is just half the battle. Accepting that help is the other half.

9. TAKE CARE OF YOURSELF IN ALL WAYS.

While regular exercise and eating right isn't necessarily going to fix your depression, these things can help you to feel better;

the converse is also true, as eating unhealthy foods and remaining sedentary is going to make you feel much worse.

Typically the last thing that any depressed person wants to do is exercise and care for themselves physically, but this is a very important part of your recovery and treatment. If you don't take care of yourself physically, your mental state will never improve.

It's also important to keep yourself connected socially and emotionally to those that are important to you. Don't give up your religious pursuits or isolate yourself from your family; don't give up your hobbies and the things that are important to you, even if you're not finding the same enjoyment you once did.

10. DON'T GIVE UP.

It's probably going to be very tempting to throw in the towel the day you actually give in to that urge to have a crying jag or the first time you snap at your child and go on that infamous guilt trip. But giving up when you have setbacks or when things don't happen the way you expect them to is a mistake.

Fighting your depression is going to be a lifetime battle with setbacks and triumphs just like anything else. But the real mistake would be to just toss in the towel and figure that it's no use.

If you keep with it, your depression will get better and you will learn healthier ways of thinking and coping. You might not ever be actually cured, but you can learn happiness and healthy thinking once again - but only if you don't give up!

Printed in Great Britain
by Amazon